PRAISE

GW00659198

'Entertaining and memorable
reworks it, making this form of communication ...

— *Financial Times*

'Ever written an email? You need this book. Ever received an email? You need this book. How I have survived for over twenty years in my profession without it by my side I do not know.'

— **Annie Gallimore,** Managing Director, ACNE London, and Director, Deloitte Digital

'Email can be powerful. But managing it – all of it – can be a nightmare. In this useful, insightful and funny book you'll learn how to free yourself from the drudgery and capitalise on all the good stuff.'

— **Gareth Williams,** non-executive director and ex-CEO, sofa.com

'Kim Arnold writes plain, easy to read, entertaining English – more than you can say of most emails, which are deadly dull and ill-written, and fail to sell. Her book is a wise investment for anyone who wants to stop boring people and start persuading them.'

— **Drayton Bird,** the world's leading authority on direct marketing

'*Email Attraction* has rediscovered the power of what's still the most common form of communication in business. Whether you're an old hand or a new entrant to the world of work, the ideas in this book can save you time, get results and – most amazingly – bring a smile to dealing with email.'

— **Simon Harper,** co-founder, LOD

R^ethink

First published in Great Britain in 2021
by Rethink Press (www.rethinkpress.com)

Illustrations by Emma-Jane Black

Kim Arnold

Email
Attraction

Get what you want
every time you hit send

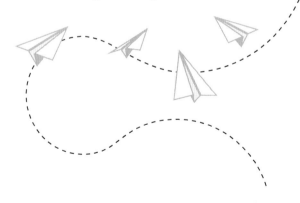

For Hope and Will

CONTENTS

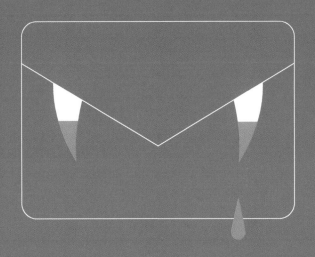

INTRODUCTION

EMAIL SUCKS SIX YEARS OF YOUR LIFE

You're likely to spend around six years of your life on email.

Yes, you heard me right. A study by Adobe in 2019 found the average white-collar worker spends around five hours on email each weekday (three or more hours of work email, two or more hours of personal email). That's over 52,000 hours on email over the course of a forty-year career (not even taking into account emailing at the weekend or post retirement).[1]

Yikes.

Just think for a moment – that's over half a decade. Over 7% of your life. A six-year commitment to email is longer than many relationships. Longer than most university degree courses. Almost as long as Christmas Day at the in-laws'.

It's longer than you spend *eating* (around four and a half years), *going on holiday* (just over three years) or *socialising* (around one year).[2]

Which means you likely spend six years of your life *complaining* about email, too (probably many more, in fact), writing things like:

- Just checking in to see if you got my email?
- So sorry to bother you again, but...
- Just wondering if you've managed to make a decision on this?

1   'Adobe email usage study' (Adobe, 2019), www.slideshare.net/adobe/2019-adobe-email-usage-study, accessed October 2020

2   G Curtis, 'Your life in numbers' (Dreams, 2017), www.dreams.co.uk/sleep-matters-club/your-life-in-numbers-infographic, accessed October 2020

- As per my last email...
- Reply, you annoying &^%$*!

And that's too darn long.

———————————— • ———————————— • ————————————

In fact, it's crazy when you think about it. You've had little or no training or support with something you spend six precious years of your life on.

———————————— • ———————————— • ————————————

But here's the good news...

Email is one of the best inventions, *ever*! Used correctly, it's your shortcut to getting people to do what you want, fast. It's an incredible communication tool that can persuade, influence and move projects forward at lightning speed (that's around 270,000 mph, by the way).

And reports of its death have been wildly exaggerated. HubSpot said in 2020 that 86% of professionals still preferred to use email when communicating for business purposes.[3]

In fact, the number of global email users is set to grow to 4.48 billion by 2024.[4]

And email is especially priceless in tough times. Times when we need to stay connected from afar, drum up new business in an economic tight spot and keep people upbeat.

Times when we need to get more done without using more money or people to help.

All you need to do is stop sending bad email. Consider this book your get-out-of-jail-free card.

3   A Hussein, '22 eye-opening statistics about sales email subject lines that affect open rates' (HubSpot, 2020), https://blog.hubspot.com/sales/subject-line-stats-open-rates-slideshare, accessed October 2020
4   'Email Statistics Report 2020–2024: Executive summary' (Radicati, 2020), www.radicati.com/wp/wp-content/uploads/2019/12/Email-Statistics-Report-2020-2024-Executive-Summary.pdf, accessed October 2020

Email is especially important when we need to get people to do what we want (employ us, promote us, give us their business, reply to our blasted email) without actually meeting in person.

Email is a low-cost (free for many, in fact), simple-to-use and easily accessible gem that's all too often overlooked. Let's turn your email into the lightning-fast shortcut it really is, so you can cut through the noise and make great stuff happen.

Be the boss of your email

If you're going to spend six years of your precious life on email, you might as well be good at it. You need to become The Inbox Emperor/ess. The Mayor/ess of Emailville. The Big Email Enchilada.

But let's not stop there. Let's cut those six years on email down to two... or even one.

Imagine thousands of hours freed up to spend on your favourite things – whether that's walking your dog, doing yoga or hanging out with your family. Wouldn't that be great?

Get more done. Have better conversations. Improve your relationships. Free up time.

As The Big Email Enchilada, you can:

- Ask for a pay rise from your harassed boss

- Get your lazy colleagues to help you on a project

- Book in client meetings quickly – no back and forth

- Motivate prospects who are flakier than a *pain au chocolat*

- Make employees complete their self-appraisals this century

- Get the Board to green light your awesome idea

- Get your invoices paid on time

Your emails should make your life *better*.

Warning: Big Email Enchilada side effects may include light-headedness, a God Complex and a completed to-do list.

Be known as the one who gets stuff done.

Do you know deep down that churning out twenty emails on autopilot isn't really a win (despite those little dopamine hits when you press send)? Do you admit that you focus on quantity over quality?

It's OK – that's all about to change.

Help is here

Your last writing help was probably at school or university. But an essay is a world away from an email. It's the difference between an eight-course tasting menu and a double espresso. The first is to be savoured and deliberated over; the second provides a quick hit with a clear purpose.

The writing you've been trained for is *not* the writing you've ended up doing. Every. Single. Day.

This book is here to put that right.

Here's some great news. When we think of efficiency and improvement, we tend to think big (and expensive).

But usually the biggest changes come from the smallest of things.

Think small. No, smaller. There you go.

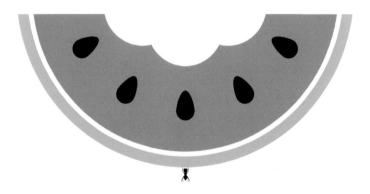

Tiny tweaks to your everyday emails bring extraordinary results.

So, are you ready? Ready to ditch the misunderstandings, frustration and years of wasted time and effort?

Ready to launch yourself into a new world of effortlessly effective email that helps you build brilliant relationships, inspires awesome action and gets some serious stuff done?

Let's do it!

TRY IT TODAY

- Remember: you've never been taught how to write effective emails (so it's no wonder you're not getting results).

- Read on to see how you can free up some of the time you spend on email to do the things you love.

- Get started today – every little improvement will make a big difference to your everyday life.

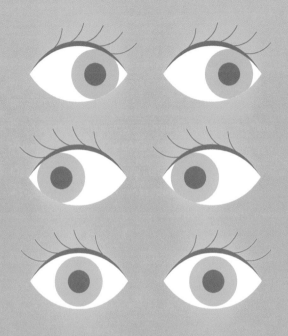

1

IT'S NOT THEM, IT'S YOU

In 1995 I lived in Russia as part of my university degree, braving a snot-freezing winter in Voronezh, an industrial town 500 km south of Moscow.

While I could make myself understood on the whole, communication sometimes broke down. Badly.

Over dinner one night, my wonderful hostess enquired (or so I thought) if I liked language.

'Yes, of course! I love languages,' I gushed. 'I'm really passionate about them. I'm studying German as well as Russian.'

She looked at me a little strangely, but with a characteristic shrug of her shoulders, she moved the conversation on.

The next morning, I sat down to breakfast with my hosts and did a double take. There, in front of me, balanced proudly atop a piece of black bread, was an enormous *tongue*.

Not a slice of tongue. Not a sliver. But a whole whopping great cow's tongue.

And then it hit me – the word 'yazyk' in Russian has two meanings – language (like 'mother tongue' in English) and, well, tongue. While I'd been banging on about my love of language, my hostess had in fact been asking if I'd like *tongue on toast for breakfast*.

Gulp.

It was clearly a delicacy that had cost them a lot of money, so there was no option but to chow down on each grisly bite with a grin. It was the longest breakfast of my life.

Are we speaking the same language?

Now of course, we expect mishaps when foreign languages are involved.

But communication screw-ups also happen when we're supposedly speaking the same language.

And that's especially true when we email.

In email, we don't have the same cues as when we talk to someone. We can't read facial expressions or body language. We can't tell if they're checking their watch and switching off, or whether they're sitting forward in their chair, eating up our every word. We can't hear their tone of voice and know whether they're excited, nervous or ready to disembowel themselves with a stapler.

Without these visual or aural clues, we just cross our fingers, pray to the email gods and hope for the best. We send our emails off into the ether with no idea what will happen next. Will we get a reply? Will we get the action we need? Who the hell knows?

And then, when we don't get a reply, or the answer we want, we start whining:

'I can't believe he didn't reply to my email.'

'They only gave me one bit of the info I asked for – argh!'

'She was so rude – I just can't believe it.'

'They won't engage with me however hard I try.'

But – and I hope you're sitting down to hear this – *it's not actually all the recipients' fault.*

Really.

Now the good news is you can end the frustrating merry-go-round and enjoy more certainty about the results you'll get from your emails. Sounds great, right?

The bad news is you've got to suck up the responsibility for the rubbish results you've been getting.

Because here's the thing – it's actually not your recipients who are the problem. It's you.

Time to get real

There's a term in information technology (IT) taught to me by my (long-suffering) tech aide: Problem In Chair Not In Computer (PICNIC). Apparently, it's commonly used by IT support-desk staff when they're rolling their eyes at simple user error. And it's the same for your emails.

Are you so busy blaming your recipients for screw-ups that you don't stop to wonder if *you're also to blame*?

In all your emails, you have a responsibility to be:

- Clear
- Interesting
- Thoughtful
- Relevant

If you're not getting the response you need, I bet you're not nailing this like you should.

The Fateful 8

You're probably making one of these eight mistakes in your emails:

 The Info Dump – overloading the recipient with bucket loads of information.

 The Workout – making people work too hard to figure out what you want them to do.

 The Maze – the next step is confusing instead of easy.

 The Shoulda-Picked-Up-The-Phone – email was the wrong call.

 The 'My Eyes, My Eyes' – ugly-as-hell email.

 The Toddler in a Sweet Shop – asking for too many things at once.

 The Hedge – giving too many options.

 The Undertaker – burying your call-to-action (CTA) (ie what you want people to do).

Over the coming chapters, I'll show you how to fix each one of these problems. But here's what you need to remember for now.

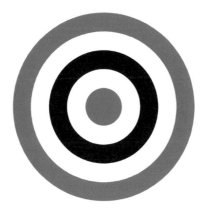

The biggest issue is that we focus on the wrong criteria for success. We hurry out email after email, without a *second thought about what we want to happen next.*

We high-five ourselves when we've sent thirty emails in a morning – no matter what results we get from them.

We value quantity, not quality. Process, not outcomes. Speed over effectiveness.

We measure the wrong things.

Don't worry, we'll fix this. But first, one final, critical lesson.

TRY IT TODAY

- Take your time when writing emails – speed is not your friend.
- Value quality over quantity.
- Focus on results, not process.

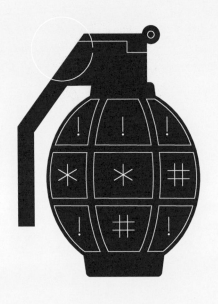

2

BEWARE THE
EMOTIONAL EMAIL

We've all been there. Steam coming out of our ears, knuckles white with anger, we've bashed out an email about something our recipient supposedly has or hasn't done.

Before we know it, we've pulled the pin and lobbed our email hand grenade into the ether. And what comes next is always an ugly explosion of reciprocated upset, resentment or anger from our recipient.

Repeat after me: *'Emotional or impulsive emails are never a good idea.'* And they're all too easy with email, where we can fire out our frustrations with just a couple of clicks and without a second's thought.

Think of the last time you sent an email when you were angry, upset, frustrated, disappointed or aggravated. Did anything good come of it? Or did you get a curt/defensive/rude/frustrated response back?

Thought so.

We've all read horror stories of people accidentally 'replying all' with snarky comments or sending rude emails to the wrong people. But emotional emails are just as dangerous.

Emails sent in a heightened emotional state can cost money, jobs or reputation. Emails sent while drunk can cost all three. Don't let that happen to you.

Remember, too, that your recipient reads your email in whatever mood they're in – so if they're already having a bad day, a loaded phrase like 'I was surprised to learn...' or 'It seems odd to me that...' can be enough to tip them over the edge.

Before you lob that grenade, try these steps:

- **Let the sun go down on your email** – wait overnight, or at least an hour or two before sending. Think about your reader and how they'll react. Will your email really help you get what you want in the longer term? Or are you just appeasing your inner child right now? Chances are, you won't feel like sending it once you've calmed down. If you still think it's worth it in the morning, at least you'll have a better grasp of the risks versus the rewards.

- **Ask yourself, 'Would I say this to their face?'** We're often a lot braver and take bigger risks sitting behind a keyboard than when we're in person with someone – but it's still the same audience. Read your email out loud to gauge your tone and understand whether you're sounding rude, passive aggressive or sarcastic.

- **Show your email to someone else with no skin in the game** – they'll be able to give you objective advice about the tone and content of your email. What might seem like a gentle reproach to you might feel like a kick in the unmentionables to someone else. And the process of talking through your frustrations with an impartial someone might just open the pressure valve enough to make your email redundant.

We'll talk more about when not to email at all in Chapter 12, but next you're going to learn how to:

- Get your head into the right space from the start, to make every email a winner.

- Replace visual and aural clues with other vital info about your recipient.

- Get more certainty about the response you'll receive to every one of your emails.

Let's dive in!

TRY IT TODAY

- Feeling emotional? Angry? Upset? Wait for at least an hour or two before you even think about writing that email!

- Think about the language and tone of your message, avoiding loaded phrases that could tip an already upset recipient over the edge.

- Imagine you're face to face with your recipient. Don't say anything or use language or tone of voice in an email that you wouldn't do in person.

- Still not sure? Get an impartial opinion on the content of your email.

3

HEY YOU! DON'T BE
THE PARTY BORE

Who do you look at first in a group photo featuring you?

Why do you automatically turn around when someone shouts, 'Hey you'?

Why do you look up when a random child screams, 'Mum' or 'Dad'? (You don't have kids? Well then, I'm as confused as you.)

We can't help it. We humans are selfish. We think about ourselves a lot.

On the plus side, this self-centredness has kept us alive as a race for thousands of years, helping us overcome sabretooth tigers, bubonic plagues and slow wifi connections. But on the downside, our egotistical ways are a *nightmare for emails*. Because if something doesn't speak to us in a nanosecond – we ignore it completely.

Which leads us to our emails and why they aren't working.

How *not* to start an email

Want to know a sure-fire way of never getting a response to your email? Start like this:

- I'm writing to introduce myself...

- I'm writing to tell you about my business...

- I'm writing to ask if you would participate in our survey...

Why is this such a killer? Well, it's all about you and nothing about the recipient.

Dong. Yes, that's your email death knell.

While you are so eager to get what *you want* (a new contact, a favour, a meeting in the diary), you haven't taken into account what *the recipient might be interested in*.

'And what's that?' you may ask.

Easy. *Themselves.*

In fact, they are likely sitting there with your email in front of them, asking, 'What's in it for me?' and 'Why the hell should I care?'

And with their groaning inbox, looming deadlines and bursting schedule crowding in from all sides, they will probably make the snap decision not to bother with your 'me, me, me' email.

It's just not that important. There's no immediate payback for them. It can wait.

Which is downright rubbish for you, by the way.

So how do we get off on the right foot with our emails? It's all about the chat.

Less me, me, me, more you, you, you

I want you to think of email as a conversation – a back and forth, a trade of ideas and words with your recipient. It's not a one-way street.

Email isn't a dumper truck you tip all your information out of, burying your reader into submission.

In the offline world, we get fed up pretty darn quickly with people who talk about themselves all the time.

We've all been stuck with the bore at the party who bangs on about their job: 'Yeah well, I'm pretty big in crypto – it's actually a super-interesting topic that not many people understand – where do I start? Well, let me take you back to the origins of Bitcoin...'

Yawwwnnnnsnoredrool.

And it's just the same in email. Too much 'I' and 'me' and not enough 'you' is a big turn-off.

But at least in the real world, we get some non-verbal cues from the person we're talking to – the tone of their voice; their facial expressions and body language. We generally know if we've got their attention or whether they'd rather be talking to someone – anyone – else.

With email, we don't have the benefit of these critical cues. Without them to guide us, we tend to fall back on what *we* are interested in instead – our needs and wants, not our reader's.

So how do we bridge the gap between us and them? To get out of our own heads and into theirs? Well, welcome to the three Ws.

The three Ws – who, what and why

Before you start writing any email, take a few seconds. Pause. Ask yourself these questions:

Who am I writing to?

What are they interested in? How do they like to communicate? Have I received an email from them – was it long or short? Formal or informal?

If you don't know the recipient, make your best guess. And make sure you're emailing the right person – if you're going after a senior executive, their assistant, chief of staff or unit head might be a much better bet.

What do I want to happen *after* I send this email?

For example, I want the recipient to:

- Make an introduction
- Give feedback on my report
- Refer me to someone else
- Give me a pay rise
- Agree to a meeting
- Reach a decision
- Forward my email
- Make a recommendation, etc

Why should they care?

What's in it for them? What's the curiosity factor? *How will my email make their life or lives better?*

If you spend just a few seconds thinking about your recipient before you start writing, you skyrocket the chances of your email being opened and replied to – a big return on investment for your time.

Let's put all this into practice with some before-and-after examples.

Getting time in a busy executive's diary

 You want to get a meeting with a CEO you haven't met before to discuss charity initiatives. She's notoriously booked up months in advance, but you've got a great idea you want to discuss with her.

Previously you might have written something like:

EXAMPLE: BEFORE

To: Megan
From: Ben
Re: CSR programme

Dear Megan

My name is Ben Morelli and I am from a company called Charity Begins At Work. I have been investigating your organisation's current charitable initiatives and I believe that there's an opportunity for you to support local charities and engage your employees more around charitable work.

I feel very passionately about our opportunity to help others less fortunate than ourselves and I would like to explore with you the idea of setting up a company-wide corporate social responsibility (CSR) programme. Please can you let me know when you have time in your diary to meet with me to talk through my ideas.

Best wishes,
Ben

Lots of 'I have been doing' and 'I feel' and 'I would like'. Not much about Megan at all.

But when Ben knows that he needs to be less 'me, me' and more 'you, you', he stops to pause before he writes. He spends a few moments thinking about Megan, applying the three Ws:

- **Who is she?** A stressed-out CEO with a diary booked solid. Her social media feeds show that she's focused on 'improving client experience' for the business. Her tweets are short and to the point.

- **What does he want her to do afterwards?** Meet with him for a discussion.

- **Why should she care?** Ben's CSR ideas would help to strengthen her relationships with clients.

So this is what he writes instead:

EXAMPLE: AFTER

Title: An idea for client relationship superglue...

Hi Megan

Your LinkedIn article on strengthening client relationships got me thinking.

Energy businesses like your clients are increasingly focusing on their charitable initiatives. They're looking to partner with vendors who have a strong track record in this area. So, I have some ideas how a CSR programme could help you, your clients and your community.

Can we grab thirty minutes to chat through this on Wednesday or Thursday next week?

Please let me know when is good for you.

Best wishes,
Ben

It's short and to the point, mirrors Megan's style and talks to her priorities, not Ben's. It starts with 'Your' to get off on the right foot. And it is formatted so it is easy to read (more on this in Chapter 5).

Asking for a case study

 You want your client to agree to participate in a case study based on a project you've recently completed with them. This is what you might have written, before you read this life-changing chapter:

EXAMPLE: BEFORE

To: Imran
From: Sarah
Re: Invitation to participate in case study

Dear Imran,

I am writing to ask if you would agree to participate in a case study with us focused around the customer relationship management (CRM) project that we implemented for you.

I hope that you will agree that the project was a success and will bring a great deal of value to the organisation going forward.

If you agree, I would interview you on the telephone as a first step. Then I would write up the transcript for your review. You would be able to send over any edits for me to incorporate, and then sign off the final version.

Please let me know if this is something that you would like to participate in.

Kind regards,
Sarah

What do you notice? Yes, that's right – lots of 'I' and not much 'you'. A focus on the benefits for Sarah and not for Imran. And it's written in a wordy, stuffy style.

Like Ben, Sarah needs to apply the three Ws:

- **Who is the target reader?** Imran, a busy middle manager of a software business. Relaxed, only ever wears jeans and t-shirts. Seems quite shy and struggles to get visibility with senior management.

- **What does she want him to do afterwards?** Agree to a case study interview.

- **Why should he care?** It could help him to promote himself internally.

EXAMPLE: AFTER

To: Imran
From: Sarah
Re: Profile raiser for you?

Hi Imran

Great to see the CRM in action and the feedback from the sales team!

You mentioned how hard it is to showcase your projects to senior management. How about we do a case study together? It'd only take an hour and could be a great tool for you to get in front of your stakeholders.

Let me know if you have time on Tuesday or Thursday morning for a quick Zoom interview.

Have a great day,
Sarah

So what's different? A much more relaxed tone of voice to suit Imran's style, a focus on the benefits for him (profile raising) and an emphasis on how little time the case study will need from him.

Much better, right?

And speaking of tone of voice, we're going to talk about this in the next chapter, because this is *the key* to getting a response from your emails. See you on the other side.

TRY IT TODAY

Use your three Ws the next time you write an email:

- Who are you writing to?

- What do you want to happen next?

- Why should they care?

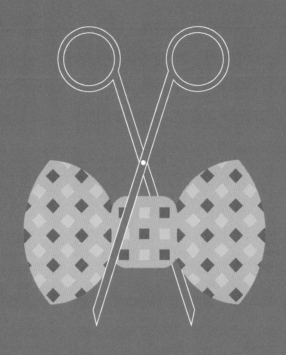

4

DITCH THE STIFF, STARCHY AND STUFFY

I vividly remember the clothes I wore as a teenager for my first day's work experience with a PR agency in London.

Itchy pinstriped polyester suit with ginormous shoulder pads and 'sensible' one-size-too-big court shoes borrowed from my mum. I recall feeling so stiff and restricted as I walked through the doors, I could barely lift my arm to shake hands.

These days, I'm immediately transported back to that buttoned-up feeling whenever I see stiff, starchy emails like this:

EXAMPLE: BEFORE

To: Meena

From: Lloyd

Re: Board presentation feedback request

Dear Meena

I am writing to request your feedback on the attached presentation. Please note, all comments should adhere to aforementioned Board presentation guidelines.

Kindly return your comments at your earliest convenience to ensure that the presentation is delivered in a timely manner.

Kind regards,

Lloyd

Ugh. Stodgier than a three-week-old bagel. Stiffer than a Brit's upper lip. It feels like it's been written by a corporate robot trying to impress his robot boss. ('Affirmative.')

Stuffy emails don't engage the reader. In fact, we ignore them.

It isn't wrong exactly, though, is it? Maybe you feel this kind of language is *expected* in your organisation – after all, everyone else does it, even your bosses. Is it really so bad?

Well yes, I'm afraid it is. And here's why.

You have to write to connect, not impress.

Stiff, stuffy, formal language creates a brick wall between you and your audience. It confuses and alienates. It gets in the way of an emotional connection – the connection that encourages your reader to act. And so stuffy emails get ignored.

I know, I know – I'm sure you want to appear intelligent and professional. But in reality, the opposite happens.

Studies show that when you use unnecessarily long words like 'aforementioned', readers think you're less intelligent, not more.[5] So perhaps these waffly words aren't so innocent after all.

---

5   D Oppenheimer, 'Consequences of erudite vernacular utilized irrespective of necessity: Problems with using long words needlessly', *Applied Cognitive Psychology*, 20 (2006), 139–156, www.ucd.ie/artspgs/semantics/ConsequencesErudite.pdf, accessed October 2020

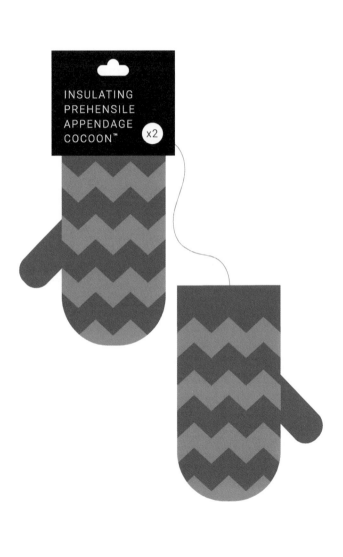

INSULATING
PREHENSILE
APPENDAGE
COCOON™ x2

Stop doctoring your words

Still need convincing to let go of formal language? Think about this scenario.

You have a headache and go to see your doctor.

She says, 'You have sphenopalatine ganglioneuralgia. It can be treated by the temporary cessation of ingesting sub-zero items.'

You might think, 'Sveno what? Sounds bad. Really bad. I'm going to die, aren't I? Argh! But I'm so young and I haven't even tried paddle-boarding yet. But what was that? Something about a treatment? In Antarctica?'

But if she says, 'You have an ice cream headache. Avoid eating really cold foods', you get it straight away. You can act more quickly. You feel reassured.

So channel your inner calm doctor with your writing. Make it easy for your audience to understand and act on your words.

Less is more

Let's rewrite the earlier email with a more informal approach:

EXAMPLE: AFTER

To: Meena

From: Lloyd

Re: Board presentation – your feedback by Friday please

Dear Meena

Here's the Board presentation for you to take a look at.

Please send me your feedback by Friday, following the guidelines I sent earlier.

Kind regards,

Lloyd

What do you notice? It's still polite and professional, but much easier to read, and warmer and more engaging in tone (useful when you're trying to get someone to do something). The subject line is much punchier, too, with a clear call-to-action (CTA) and deadline.

Depending on your work culture and your recipient, you could be even more conversational and swap the 'Dear' for 'Hi' and 'Kind regards' for 'Many thanks' or 'Best wishes'.

(More on greetings and sign-offs in Chapter 6, and subject lines in Chapter 11.)

But a word of warning – you also need to watch out for those cheesy old business clichés, like 'take that offline' and 'manage the optics'.

We all say we hate them, but when our fingers hover over the keyboard, the spirit of the corporate world can suddenly overtake us. Like a Ouija board at a séance, the letters take on a life of their own, and before we know it, we've shifted a paradigm, boiled the ocean and moved the needle all before lunchtime.

Now you may say, 'Everyone else uses them' and 'They're just part of our work culture'. But simple, everyday language will always connect better with your audience.

So watch out for the phrases that make your emails sound insincere.

But how else can we make our emails sound less stuffy?

Don't be a Karen or Damian at the party

Think of the last office party you went to. I know, it might have been a while ago. Who did you enjoy talking to?

It probably wasn't Damian from customer support who'd had way more than his allocated two house cocktails and was spilling the beans on his lusty affair with Jason from the post room; nor was it Karen from finance with her jacket still on at midnight, lecturing you on how accountants are so frequently misunderstood.

You probably warmed to Middle-Ground Myra, who was warm and easy to talk to, but not over the top.

That's exactly the tone you want for your writing. Professional doesn't have to be stuffy. Informal isn't the same as sloppy.

You want to aim for conversational. Use the words you'd normally use when you speak to someone in person.

Six tips for a more conversational tone:

1. **Use contractions** – 'it's' instead of 'it is' and 'you're' instead of 'you are'.

2. **Swap jargon-y business words like 'utilise' and 'commence' for their easier-going cousins 'use' and 'start'.**

3. **Avoid the passive voice** – 'Employees are invited to participate' – and use the active voice instead – 'We'd like you to take part'.

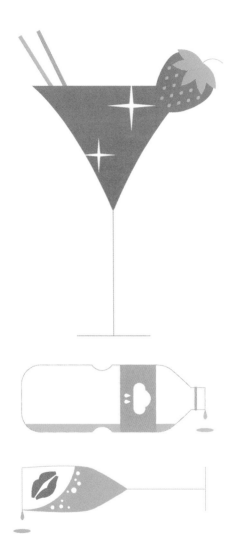

4. **Use 'we' and 'you' to create connection** – it's like saying someone's name.

5. **Ditch old-fashioned filler words and phrases** like 'with regard to', 'needless to say', 'it is important to note', 'for all intents and purposes' and 'at all times'.

6. **Don't be afraid to break the rules** – despite what your English teacher said at school, you *can* start sentences with 'and' and 'because', and/or use sentence fragments, eg *'Why? Because Q2 is looking soft.'*

The ultimate test for your emails

If you wouldn't say it, don't write it. Here's how you test it:

Read it out loud.

If you stumble over any words, they're too long or formal. If you wince a little when you say something, you need to loosen up your language.

Yes, if you're in an open-plan workspace, people might think you've got an imaginary friend, but it's worth it. I promise.

TRY IT TODAY

- Use short, simple words you'd use in conversation.
- Start a sentence with 'and' (you rebel).
- Try a contraction like 'it's', 'I'm' or 'we're'.

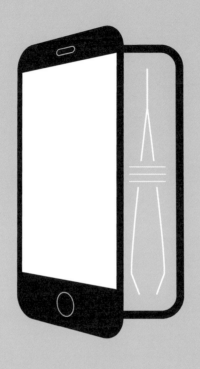

5

OUCH! YOUR EMAILS NEED TWEEZER TIME

I'm partial to a Michelin-starred meal on occasion. Scallops and yuzu foam? Oh, go on then. Ganache with chocolate soil? Twist my arm.

We can learn a lot from those fancy chefs, because they know a thing or two about winning customers over.

They know that they need to appeal to our eyes as well as to our taste buds – we start judging their food visually before we've taken the first bite.

And that's why chefs painstakingly tweeze micro-herbs on to our ceviche and spin sugar domes to sit on top of our panna cotta. If they don't create instant visual appeal on our plate, we post pictures of their nasty greying steak on TripAdvisor before we've even left the restaurant.

And this tweezer philosophy is exactly the same for your emails.

Yes, your messages need to be punchy and clear (we'll come to that soon), but first of all your emails need to *look* good. Otherwise your readers won't get past the first 'Hi'.

In fact, I bet you opened up an email just this week that made you want to gouge your eyes out with a spoon – and that's *before* you even read the first word. You've probably already forgotten the content of that stodgy, overwhelming block of text that you shut down immediately and filed away to read at a later date (aka when hell freezes over).

So how do you prettify and simplify your emails to make them irresistibly tempting to your recipients? Well, you need to create some space.

Heavenly spaces

I was speechless when I visited one of my clients' offices.
The lobby was so cavernous, you could have parked
Air Force One in it. Or Richard Branson's ego. Almost.

The towering glass atrium shot up twenty storeys.
Stunning white marble glistened from every wall and floor.
It was breathtaking, like heaven would be depicted in a film.
I half expected the reception staff to have wings.

Most of the lobby wasn't even being used – just a few chairs and plants strategically dotted around. *The rest was left beautifully and decadently empty.*

There was such luxury to dedicating so much space to... well, space. It conveyed a wonderful sense of calm and stillness.

It also felt important.

And it's just the same for our writing.

There's a huge value to white space on the page because it allows our important words to stand out.

It allows our messages to breathe.

Long sentences and long paragraphs in small fonts stuffed on to the page can have the opposite effect because they create a sense of overwhelm, chaos and confusion before we've read a word. It's like a wall of words that the reader will need crampons and a grappling hook to climb – and most will give up right at the start. Cramming so many words in a tight space feels claustrophobic and oppressive – like the wordy equivalent of *The Hoarder Next Door*. This isn't even a very long paragraph, but I bet you're finding it harder to read than what came before, because the sentences themselves are much longer, there's less white space and it's taking more brainpower to read them, and that feels like hard work which you don't really need any more of right now, thank you very much, because you've got enough on your plate and you just need to get to the point.

Phew. See what I mean?

The next time you sit down to write, remember the value of the heavenly white space on your page to draw your reader in and to get your message across.

How to give your readers room to breathe

Use these six steps to make your emails irresistible to read:

1. **Start with a short first sentence.** It's an easy entry point for the reader, indicating this won't be a difficult email to get through.

2. **Use short sentences throughout.** Ideally sixteen words or fewer (harder than you may think). If you must use a longer sentence, think how you can break it up with brackets, colons or hyphens.

3. **Use short paragraphs with plenty of clear space between them.**

4. **Change your line spacing from 1 to 1.15 or 1.5.** Most email providers will let you do this quite easily in your top toolbar – it makes a huge difference to ease of reading.

5. **Think about how your recipient might read your email:** on mobile, desktop or tablet. Your email might look fine when it's stretched across your fancy 34" widescreen monitor, but on your recipient's mobile, it might look like an essay. So, reduce the size of the window that you draft your email in – right down to mobile phone size if you can. You'll then be able to judge how your email will look to your audience.

6. **Keep your font size legible** – 12 pt for emails is ideal.

EXAMPLE: BEFORE

To: Laura

From: Bethan

Re: Wellbeing For Women Conference Follow-Up

Dear Laura

I very much enjoyed meeting with you and your colleagues last Tuesday at the afternoon breakout session at the Wellbeing For Women conference and our discussions around women with imposter syndrome. I would like to continue our conversation about coaching for women with confidence issues as I think this is an often-overlooked area for many businesses, but one that can reap many benefits for both the women themselves as well as the businesses that they work in. We have done extensive research into this area that we can share with you and we would like to get your views on our statistics to see if they are in line with what you are seeing. Are you free on Friday at 2pm to meet at your offices? I think we could have some interesting discussions and look forward to meeting up soon to talk this through in detail.

Regards,
Bethan

What's wrong with this email?

- The font is too small.

- The first sentence is too long.

- The paragraph is too big and bulky.

- The second sentence is forty-six words – way too long.

- The CTA gets lost in body of text (more on this in Chapter 10).

- Tight line spacing.

EXAMPLE: AFTER

To: Laura

From: Bethan

Re: Imposter syndrome – so much more to talk about!

Dear Laura

Great to meet you at the wellbeing conference last week.

I'd love to continue our chat about imposter syndrome: why it's an overlooked area and how coaching can help both women and their organisations. I can share new research on the subject and would welcome your thoughts.

Is Friday at 2pm good to meet at your offices?

Best wishes,

Bethan

What's right with this email?

- The short first sentence in a single paragraph makes it easy to start reading.

- The longer sentence is broken up with a colon.

- There's only key information included.

- Clear call-to-action – ends on what Bethan wants the recipient to *do* (more on this in Chapter 10).

So always remember to give your readers some heavenly spaces in your emails – they'll think you're an angel if you do.

TRY IT TODAY

- Start your email with a short first sentence.
- Keep paragraphs to 2-3 sentences max, with lots of white space between them.
- Use generous line spacing and font size throughout.

6

WHOA! DON'T RUSH THOSE SUBJECT LINES AND GREETINGS

Step away from the subject line. I repeat. Step. Away. From. The. Subject. Line.

Easy, tiger. I know you're eager to get going, but *do not* start with your subject line.

Writing your headline before your email is like choosing your dessert with your aperitif – you don't know what you're going to be in the mood for just yet. Or deciding on your degree before you've finished pre-school – you don't know how it's going to turn out right now.

Your subject line is one of the most vital bits of your email. Don't rush it.

You might have written an email sent from the gods – succinct, witty and oh-so-persuasive – but call it 'Update' or 'June Newsletter' and you might as well have not bothered.

No one will open it.

So hold your horses and wait until Chapter 11 where we get down and dirty into the art of writing subject lines that get your emails opened as often as possible.

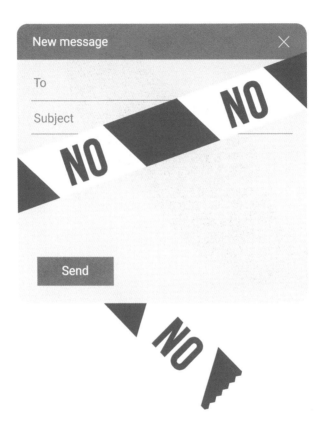

Greetings, earthlings

You might wonder about what greeting to use at the *start of your emails*.

Well, don't. You're a grown adult who manages to greet people successfully every day.

You buy your morning mocha-chocca-two-shot-cino without worrying about how to greet your barista. You call up your clients or colleagues without worrying what to say at the start.

So, unless you're reading this in prison for public indecency, you already know what's an appropriate greeting.

Email is no different from real life.

Still fretting about starting your email on the right note?
Ask yourself these questions:

How would you greet this person if you met them in real life? Would you kiss them on both cheeks, go in for the bear hug or hang back with a handshake?

What kind of person are they? How formal are they? Are they a jeans-and-trainers kind of person, or are they never seen without pinstripes and brogues? What industry do they work in? What culture are they from? What greeting do they use in their emails to you?

What kind of person are you? How formal or informal are you with people? Make sure you're consistent in the tone of your emails – you don't have to go all buttoned-up just because you're writing. If you're a luvvie PR princess, you might well get away with 'Hello darling' in a client email. Or if you're a shorts-wearing IT developer, 'Hey Peter' might be fine. But if you're a corporate lawyer, you might find 'Hi Sarah' relaxed enough, thank you very much.

 What's the context? If you're delivering bad news (not always best done over email, but sometimes you must), don't start with 'Hey there!' – 'Hi X' or 'Dear X' would be better (and definitely don't use an exclamation after 'Hi'). If you're trying to get your team pumped up about a new project, 'Dear valued team member' is an instant vibe killer. They will probably think they're getting the heave-ho. Maybe you could let rip instead with a 'Hey everyone – great news!'

Thinking about these questions helps you choose the right greeting for your particular email.

For most of us, a simple 'Hi X' is fine. Use 'Dear' if you have to be more formal (but it's pretty rare these days).

Just use your initiative. You've got this, smarty pants.

How to end on the right note

The same questions apply when you sign off your email.
Think about your recipient, your context and your personality to
decide what's right for your specific email and reader.

Don't use an automatic sign-off for every email. Especially if
it's the uber-lazy 'KR' (as an abbreviation for 'kind regards').
If you can't even be bothered to type out your sign-off, your
reader may wonder what else you cut corners on.

**Automatic sign-offs make your
emails feel generic and rushed.
Whereas you want them to feel
warm, genuine and intimate.**

'Best wishes', 'Speak soon' (if you are in fact going to talk
imminently) or 'Many thanks' are often good middle-ground
sign-offs.

For quick, informal emails, you can just sign your name.
That's OK, too.

If you want to be more formal, by all means crack open a 'Kind regards', but don't default to it. And if your relationship with your recipient deepens, change your sign-off to suit. If you're still 'kind regarding' someone you've sunk ten pints in the pub with, find something more informal.

So greetings and sign-offs aren't as hard as you may have thought, right? In the next chapter, I'm going to introduce you to the juicy *HEC Hamburger Technique* – it's a recipe you won't want to miss.

TRY IT TODAY

- Think about your recipient and context when choosing greetings and sign-offs.
- Ditch automatic sign-offs.
- Don't start with your subject line.

7

MMMM... INTRODUCING THE HEC HAMBURGER TECHNIQUE

This chapter might make your stomach rumble, but it'll be worth it.

It's an introduction to my no-brainer three-part formula for writing brilliant emails. Every. Single. Time.

The following chapters go into more detail, but here's a bite-sized sample to get you going.

H is for hook.

This is your top bun. It's got to look enticing enough for your reader to want to take a bite (read the rest of your email).

E is for explanation.

This is the meat of your email (or your plant-based alternative, of course). It's where you fill your audience up with just the right amount of tasty information.

C is for call-to-action (CTA).

This is your bottom bun, which makes it easy to pick up your burger and start chomping.

Listen – you need to write HEC Hamburger emails.

Without this recipe, everything is sloppy and hard to get a hold of. Being clear about what you want people to do is critical if you want them to digest every bite of your email.

Email is kind of an emeal!

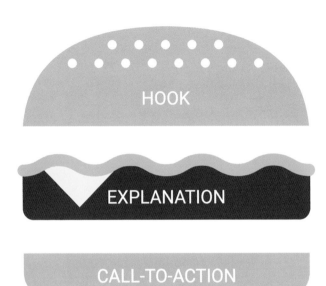

Why is the HEC Hamburger Technique so darn tasty? Well, it gets you off autopilot and makes you structure and work through your emails in a more thoughtful, effective way.

It turns all your activity into action.

And it helps you get results from all those hours spent on email.

EXAMPLE OF AN HEC HAMBURGER EMAIL

To: All Employees

From: Ciaran, HR

Re: Easier appraisals

[Hook — get the recipient interested] Appraisals are going to be a whole lot easier this year.

[Explanation — share critical information] Next week you'll be sent a new appraisal form that's quicker and simpler to fill in. There's a 360 option, where you can ask for feedback from colleagues with just a click.

[CTA — what do you want them to do?] Watch out for the form in your inbox next week with more information.

Many thanks

Ciaran

Head on over to the next chapter to get started – how to write your perfect hook with the perfect bait to reel in your reader.

TRY IT TODAY

Think about every email having three distinct parts:

- Hook
- Explanation
- Call-to-action (CTA)

8

HOW TO AVOID
SOUL-SUCKING HOOKS

So now that you've been introduced to the HEC Hamburger Technique, let's get started with your *hook* – the top bun of your burger and the first line of your email after your greeting.

A great hook is the difference between your email being read straight away or trashed or consigned to 'read later' (ie never).

Most emails hit the trash before they are ever read.

What makes a great hook? Well, it's not 'I hope you're well'. Instead, it's:

- Loaded with the perfect bait to lure each specific reader in
- Bite-sized and easy to get a hold of
- Irresistibly tasty, creating curiosity

Get it right, and your reader is so well hooked they can't help but read the rest of your email. But screw it up within the first line, and you might as well not have bothered writing another word.

Hook horrors

I suspect right now you don't focus on your hook much, if at all. You probably dash off this crucial first sentence like you're writing a shopping list or a passive-aggressive note to the neighbour who keeps blocking your driveway. In fact, that note would likely get to the point much faster than the emails you send now.

Do you trot out a bland platitude without engaging your brain, as you're so eager to get to the main point of your email?

But there is no main point if no one reads it.

I wonder if you've been guilty of one of these hook horrors?

The Hook Horror Hall Of Fame

- **I hope this email finds you well** – what else can your email do? Tap dance? Extra points deducted for being weirdly formal.

- **As per my last email** – congratulations, Mr/Ms Passive Aggressive, you've given me a guilt trip in just five words.

- **I hope you're well** – blander than a bowl of quinoa.

- **I hope your well** – need to bleach my eyeballs. (We'll chat about grammar in Chapter 13. It's important.)

- **Allow me to introduce myself** – no, you're not a Count at a Viennese ball trying to woo a debutante. And by the way, I don't care who you are (remember Chapter 3 – it's not about you).

- **I have an offer you can't refuse** – oh yes, I can. I really can.

- **I'm Prince Rahim from the Kingdom of Duban seeking your help with a money transfer** – just no.

- **Feeling lonely? Need some company in your area?** Er... let's stop there.

We were all forced to focus more on our hooks in the pandemic, so we didn't come across as insensitive in the middle of a global crisis. But instead of a personalised hook (more on this to come), many people just trotted out a new bland and generic opener, like:

- I hope this email finds you well in these unprecedented times.

- I hope you're well in these uncertain times.

It can be hard to know what to say, but a generic opener is rarely the right choice if you want to make a connection with your reader. It just doesn't feel personal.

Three seconds till impact

So now you understand *why you should never throw away your first line*, we can start to learn from the best.

And no one understands the power of a strong start better than email marketers. They spend thousands of hours and pounds analysing and testing the best openers to get their emails read and responded to.

Statistics show you have fewer than three seconds to grab a reader's attention in a marketing email.[6]

Just three seconds before they think about groceries, lunch or their latest Netflix addiction.

You need to think like a marketer, too – after all, you're likely trying to get your reader to act, just like they are.

6   J Nelson, 'Email marketers have only 12 words to capture readers', *Email Marketing Daily* (2015), www.mediapost.com/publications/article/263138/email-marketers-have-only-12-words-to-capture-readers.html, accessed October 2020

How to write your perfect hook

The first line of your email must do five key things.

 ## 1. Create a connection

Wherever possible, personalise your hook to your reader. Make it unique to them so they know you've spent time thinking about them. None of the openers in the 'Hook Horror Hall Of Fame' are personal – they could have been written for anyone with a pulse.

So instead of a generic 'I hope you're well', refer to something you know about the recipient, eg 'Did you get sunshine on the coast at the weekend?'

You'll see many of the most effective hooks start with or include the word 'you' or 'your'. And many of the least effective use 'I'. Make it all about the recipient.

 ## 2. Be easy to digest

Make your hook a short single sentence. This brevity whispers to your reader, 'Hey! Don't you worry – this isn't *War and Peace*. It's an easy read – see how quickly you can get started.'

Remember: rambling is gambling. Keep it short and sweet, like: 'Here's the info you needed.'

3. Create curiosity

Not being a bore is an underrated skill in email writing. In fact, *in any writing.* Let's face it, openers like *'I hope you're well'* are the email equivalent of a limp handshake. They suggest that what's next is staler than the crackers left over from Christmas. And no one wants a dry piece of that.

An exciting, intriguing hook is the opposite – fresh and enticing: 'I couldn't help but think of you when I saw this today.' It immediately grabs the reader's attention and makes them want more.

 ## 4. Make the reader *feel* something

A great hook (and I'll share some examples with you in a moment) induces emotion. After all, emotion is what causes people to *act* (or, in the case of emails, keep reading).

So think about what emotion you want your reader to feel as they start your email. Do you want to intrigue, excite or cheer them? Maybe you need to shock or surprise? Or perhaps you want them to feel relieved that you've solved all their problems.

Whatever the emotion is that you want to convey, be clear on what you want.

5. Be informal

One of the many reasons 'I hope this email finds you well' is so bad is because it's stiff and formal.

Only use openers you'd say to someone in person. In fact, if you're short on ideas, ask yourself, 'What would I say to this person if I met them on the street?'

Easy email hooks you can steal

Here are twenty-four hooks in eight different categories to get you started.

The warm and fuzzy

Use with: people you know well:

- Hope your daughter had fun at her birthday party.
- Are you feeling better?
- Did you survive the webinar marathon last week?

The connector

Use with: people you want to get closer to:

- Sarah Edwards suggested I get in touch.
- I see you're a [insert sport team] fan like me.
- I saw your blog on customer behaviour – agree with your point on diversity.

The instant gratification

Use with: busy people:

- Here's the data you asked for.
- I can help with your presentation problem.
- I have the answer to your question on X.

The shock jock

Use with: hard-to-reach people (if you don't mind taking a risk):

- You won't like this...
- Last time I said this to someone, they fired me.
- You might think I'm crazy, but...

The tease

Use with: people who you need to get excited about something:

- Well, this came as a surprise!
- You're going to love this.
- I have an idea for you.

The straight to the point

Use with: people who don't mince their words:

- We can solve the tech issues, but not until Friday.
- I've secured the meeting for next month.
- I want to introduce you to X.

The all about them

Use with: people with loads of confidence (and ego):

- I noticed you recently did X.
- This reminded me of you.
- I'd love your advice on...

The riddler

Use with: people with short attention spans:

- Did you know [interesting statistic]?
- Had your coffee yet?
- How do you feel about X?

So, now I've got you hooked on the best email openers, it's time to move on to the meat of your HEC Hamburger email: the expansion. See you in the next chapter!

TRY IT TODAY

- Start your email with a short sentence that grabs attention.
- Ditch the generic openers and make it specific to your recipient.
- Get creative!

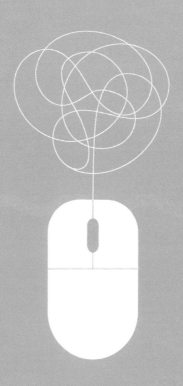

9

E IS FOR EXPLANATION

Or what the hell is your point?

If you've ever worked for a large organisation, at some point you've probably had an email like this:

EXAMPLE

To: Management team

From: Rahul, CEO

Re: Board meeting last week

Dear Team,

At last week's Board meeting, there was a discussion around taking steps to adapt the way that we approach our processes in order to keep pace with market conditions. In line with other changes being rolled out throughout the organisation, we are committed to ensuring that we are a future-ready business and we look forward to your support in making this happen.

Kind regards,

Rahul, CEO

You're likely left thinking 'Whaaaat?', scratching your head and wondering whether it was all a terrible dream.

'What did it say? Something about being future-ready? About processes? What on earth does that mean for me? Do I have to do anything? Arghhhhhhhh!'

(Or, more likely, you didn't get beyond the first dullsville sentence.)

Either way, you haven't got a clue what it all meant. It's a total waste of an email. The CEO might as well have written it in hieroglyphics and strapped it to the back of a camel – it couldn't have been any more confusing and slow.

The sad truth is, we don't just receive these kinds of emails all the time. We *send* them, too. I know, I know, that hurt.

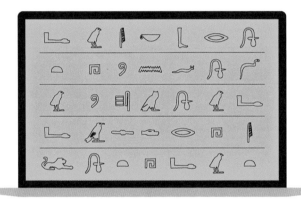

We don't mean to, of course. We think the point we're making is clear. Obvious, in fact. *Because we find it clear.*

But here's the thing: if your reader finds it unclear, then it is unclear (no matter what you think). The responsibility for making sure emails are understood sits with you, the author. Not with the reader.

In other words, communication isn't about what you write. It's how other people understand it.

Communication sent does not equal communication received.

A meaty explanation

So, how do you make sure what you write gets understood? How do you make your point clear and compelling, so it gets read and acted on?

It's time to focus on the E of your HEC Hamburger Technique – the explanation, or the meat of what you're saying.

Your explanation is a single paragraph that comes *directly after your one-sentence hook*. It's enough to chew on, but not enough to give you indigestion.

Your explanation should include:

- One main point
- Only relevant information
- Three short sentences
- What's in it for the reader

Three examples of effortless explanations

EXAMPLE 1

Hi Rochelle

Great news! *[Strong hook — who can resist good news?]*

The exec team has given the green light to your resourcing
project – they were impressed by your proposal. We now need
to develop a detailed project plan for their next meeting.
*[Explanation — gets straight to the point. Only includes strictly relevant
information. Focuses on one topic.]*

Please send me your draft plan, broken down by territory,
by 12pm on Friday 31st. *[Clear CTA — you'll learn more about this
in the next chapter.]*

Cheers,

Evan

EXAMPLE 2

Hi Niamh

Lorna Blake suggested I get in touch with you about the Digital
Marketing Manager position. *[Strong hook — leads with point of
connection, Lorna Blake.]*

You say in your job description you need someone with guerrilla
marketing experience. That's exactly what I do as Marketing
Executive with Starcomms International, for clients like
Atomic Drinks. In fact, I tick all ten boxes for your desired skills

and experience – I've attached my CV. *[Explanation: three short sentences, answering "What's in it for me?" for Niamh, leads with 'you' not 'I', includes only essential information.]*

I'm happy to pop over to your offices one lunchtime next week if you'd like to chat further. *[Clear CTA with a polite but helpful next step.]*

Best wishes

Anthony

EXAMPLE 3

Hi Liam

Great to meet you last week – that's quite a view from your office! *[Hook with a personal touch.]*

Here's my proposal to help you nail your sales strategy. *[Explanation – sometimes one sentence is enough if it answers "What's in it for me?" so clearly.]*

I'll call you as agreed on Friday to chat through. *[Clear CTA – more on this soon.]*

Best wishes,

Amani

Now you may be thinking, 'That's OK for other people, Kim, but my point is much too complicated/important/critical/complex/ sexy/lofty/erudite/fancy/exciting/cool* to be reduced into just three sentences.'

---

*delete as appropriate.

Well, here's the sucker punch for you…

If you can't explain your point in a couple of sentences, then you probably don't understand it well enough.

Because that's often the problem, isn't it? *We don't know exactly what it is that we want to say.* What our point is. What we want people to know.

So we use waffly-word-salad to disguise the lack of clarity in our thinking.

Almost everything can be reduced to a few key sentences if we try hard enough – shorter is definitely sweeter.

Data suggests the ideal length of a sales email is between 50 and 125 words (emails this length had response rates above 50%).[7] And just like salespeople, you want readers to respond to your email, too.

And, if you've applied the three Ws that we explored in

---

7   'Email length best practices for email marketers and email newbies' (Campaign Monitor, 2020), www.campaignmonitor.com/blog/email-marketing/2020/02/email-length-best-practices-for-email-marketers-and-email-newbies, accessed October 2020

Chapter 3, your explanation should be easy to write in three short sentences.

In case you need a recap, here they are again:

- *Who am I writing to?* What are they interested in?
- *What do I want to happen after I send this email?*
- *Why should they care?* What's in it for them?

Still struggling?

OK – so you've done your three Ws and you *still* think you need more than three short sentences in your explanation. Well, I'm not rolling over just yet.

I get that it's much harder to be brief than wordy. It takes time and effort. But brevity gets results. And rambling is gambling, remember?

So try one or more of these things to cut down your word count and tighten up your writing:

 Make it short and tweet

Try writing your explanation as an old-school tweet of just 140 characters – what would it say? This process forces you to prioritise only the most important information.

Once you have your tweet explanation, I bet you'll realise it's beautifully concise and you don't need any more words.

 Get your scissors out

Cut out filler words like definitely, actually, that, very, etc.

Use contractions – it's instead of it is, we're instead of we are, etc. This has the added benefit of making your writing more conversational, as we discussed in Chapter 4.

Use shorter words to replace longer ones – use, not utilise; fit, not accommodate. Again, this sounds more informal and friendly, less like you have a stick up your backside.

 **Sum it up**

Include a three-sentence executive summary in your email as your explanation, and then paste the rest of the detail into an attachment for those who need it.

 Don't use full sentences

Use bullet points for questions and key points instead of full sentences.

Rethink your approach

Ask yourself if an email really is the best medium for you right now (see Chapter 12 for more on this). Would a phone call/ presentation/ video conference be far more effective than trying to shoehorn everything into an email?

Or maybe you're trying to cover too many points in one email – do you need two or more emails over a period of a few days? Overwhelming people with too much too soon rarely works.

With all of these techniques in place, you can now write an awesome explanation that gets straight to the point. Remember, no one ever said, 'I wish that email had been longer', now, did they?

So head straight on over to Chapter 10 to find out more about calls-to-action. (And yes, you were just smacked with a CTA!)

TRY IT TODAY

- Make only one point per email.

- Cut out all non-essential information. (Be ruthless!)

- Think short and tweet (just 140 characters).

10

CONQUER YOUR
CALL-TO-ACTION

So you've nailed the start and the middle of your email – your hook and explanation. Now it's time to look at the end.

And strangely – this is the part that many people fizzle out on. They work hard on the email, and then choke on the last step.

They might worry about being too direct or coming across as bossy, and so soften their request with 'If you don't mind...' or 'Could you possibly...?' The result – a mushy email that the reader doesn't know what to do with.

Or they rush to press send and get the email out, ignoring the fact that they end with a whimper instead of a bang.

The end of your email is where you get to ask for what you want. And you need to be as clear and direct as you can.

In the marketing world, it's called a 'call-to-action' – the 'C' of your HEC Hamburger Technique. It's a persuasive invitation to your reader to take a desired action. And it's your first-class ticket to getting important stuff done.

When you conquer your CTA, it's going to feel like magic.

You mean I can actually send an email, and then people will do what I want them to do?

Well, yes. Yes, you can.

No more frustrated chasing and passive-aggressive 'As per my last email' messages. You'll have so much more free time for wild swimming, stamp collecting or a lover half your age.

To master your CTA, you need to do two things well:

1. Be clear on what you want to happen next.

The biggest problem with CTAs occurs in the thinking process. Or rather, the lack of it. We dash off emails in super-quick time just so we can tick off our list, without thinking about what we want to happen next (ie the important bit).

Remember in Chapter 3, we covered the three Ws (who, what, why). Your 'what' is for 'What do you want to happen next?' So make sure you're crystal clear on this *before* you write your CTA. Because if you're not clear on what you want the recipient to do, you can be sure as hell they won't have a clue either.

2. Make the next step easy for your recipient.

Your reader is likely short on time, patience and tolerance for wordy waffle. They don't want to spend time poring over your email with a magnifying glass to identify what they need to do next. They'll just shut it down and move on to something easier.

Remember – we're hardwired as humans to tackle the things that are easiest first. Just look at your to-do list if you don't believe me. I bet there are a few tricky items that have been hanging around since the dawn of time because they just feel like too much hard work.

Wherever possible, allow your recipient to reply in just a single sentence. Or better still, a yes or a no. I promise they will love you for it.

And if you make the next step easy for your reader, you'll see a huge boost in response rates.

A strong email CTA:

- Asks for one thing only
- Is direct and doesn't beat around the bush
- Offers a clear, specific and manageable next step
- Has a timeframe
- Is short – one sentence ideally (two–three max)

CTA makeovers

 Makeover 1: The Hide and Seek

EXAMPLE: BEFORE

To: Sean

From: Ines

Re: Feedback on annual report following our meeting

Hi Sean

I hope you're well.

Following our meeting last week to discuss our annual report, here's the draft report for your feedback. You'll see that there are different sections on each department and several recommendations at the end. I also have a question about whether or not we should include a section on impact investment, but perhaps this is too early stage to include this year.

I'll be discussing the report with the management team next week, and then cascading throughout team leaders over the coming months.

Regards,

Ines

What's wrong with this CTA?

- **It's buried in the email** ('feedback' and 'I have a question') instead of being at the end. By the time Sean has finished reading the email, he'll have forgotten what Ines is asking for.

- **It's vague** – what do 'I have a question' and 'feedback' mean? Give detailed written feedback, line by line? Give a quick glance and see if it looks broadly OK? Proofread and check for typos? Or just answer the vague question?

- **There's no deadline** – the deadliest sin of all.

So how could we rewrite this to make the CTA more compelling?

EXAMPLE: AFTER

To: Sean

From: Ines

Re: Annual report: Section 5 edits by COP Friday pls

Hi Sean

Here's the draft summary report we discussed for your feedback.

I'll discuss it with the management team next week, and after that with team leaders.

Please email me any edits you'd like to make to Section 5 by close of day on Friday.

Regards,

Ines

PS. There was a question raised about whether we should include a section on impact investment. My recommendation is that it is too early stage this time round. Let me know if you disagree.

What did Ines change? She:

- Replaced the hook with a stronger opener – it's clear what she wants

- Moved the CTA from the middle to the end of the email

- Offered a clear and manageable next step ('Email changes to Section 5')

- Used a strong, specific verb ('email')

- Offered a clear recommendation about the additional section, rather than a vague question (by the way, a PS is the most frequently read part of any email)

- Added a deadline

 ## Makeover 2: The Hedge Better

EXAMPLE: BEFORE

To: Juan

From: Michael

Re: Change Management Transformation Programme

Dear Juan

Dominique Talbot suggested I get in touch with you. I've been working with her team recently to help with change management and she thought you might find it useful to talk with me about your upcoming transformation programme.

It would be great to talk this week on the phone or video call. Alternatively, I could pop over to your office next week or the week after. Please let me know what works best for you and your schedule. Or we could meet for a coffee somewhere central, if that's easiest for you.

Kind regards,

Michael

What's wrong with this CTA?

Too. Many. Options. Argh!

Yes, it's clear that Michael wants to speak to Juan, but he gives far too many options. Phone, video call, office meeting or coffee meeting; a choice of three different weeks for the meeting – it's overwhelming.

The next step is not obvious, and Juan is likely not to reply as it feels like too much hard work.

So how does Michael make it easier for Juan to reply?

EXAMPLE: AFTER

To: Juan

From: Michael

Re: 10-min chat re: transformation programme?

Dear Juan

Dominique Talbot suggested I get in touch with you.

I've been working with her team recently to help with change management. She thought you might find it useful to talk with me about your upcoming transformation programme.

Are you free on Thursday afternoon or Friday morning for an initial phone chat?

Kind regards,

Michael

What did Michael change? He:

- Separated the hook from the explanation (easier to read as first paragraph is now short and bite-sized)

- Narrowed down the suggested format of meetings to just a phone call

- Offered two specific times to speak, making the next step simple for Juan

Makeover 3: The Too Many Cooks

EXAMPLE: BEFORE

To: All employees

From: Johnny

Re: Holiday party this year

Hi team

December will be here before we know it, so we need to decide details for our holiday party this year. We need to agree on the theme, venue and client guest list.

Please can you go to the employee portal to log your vote for the venue. You will see that there are many different options ranging from a sit-down dinner to bowling or a boat trip. We also need you to discuss your client list within your team and agree a final list of clients that you'd like to invite. Please submit this list to me no later than Thursday 28 October. You can also log your vote for the theme of the party on the employee portal, if you click on the 'Vote theme' button.

Please let me know if you have any questions or other ideas for the party – we want to make this our best yet!

KR,

Johnny

What's wrong with this CTA?

My eyes! My eyes! There are no fewer than seven CTAs in this email:

- Vote for the venue
- Discuss client list
- Agree client list
- Submit client list
- Vote for theme of party
- Ask questions
- Share ideas

If you send an email like this, you'll be lucky if the recipients do even one of these things.

So how could Johnny do it better? He should divide it up into two or more emails – the first one about the theme and venue of the party (because the reader has to go to the same place to vote for these actions), and another about the client lists.

The first one might look like this:

EXAMPLE: AFTER

To: All employees

From: Johnny

Re: Holiday party: have your say!

Hi team

It's nearly party time!

December will be here before we know it. So, we need to decide the theme and venue for our holiday party. There are lots of different options on the table, ranging from a sit-down dinner to a boat trip.

To have your say, please log your votes on the <u>employee portal</u> by Thursday 21 October.

Best wishes,

Johnny

What did Johnny change? He:

- Included a short fun hook before giving the details
- Provided more information in the explanation, without overwhelming the recipient
- Made the CTA short, clear and concise, asking for one thing (go to employee portal)
- Included a hyperlink to make it easy for people to click and take action
- Used strong, direct verb ('log')
- Included a deadline
- Subject line reinforces the CTA

Help – I have too many things to ask

If you absolutely must ask for more than one thing in an email, put them in a numbered list separated by theme. So the previous email might look like this.

EXAMPLE: AFTER

To: All employees

From: Johnny

Re: Holiday party: have your say!

Hi team

It's nearly party time!

We need to start organising our holiday party. We want you to have your say on the different options (ranging from a sit-down dinner to boat party).

Here's what we need you to do:

1. Log on to the employee portal and vote for your favourite theme and venue by Thursday 21 October

2. Email me a final list of clients you'd like to invite by EOD Thursday 28 October.

Best wishes,

Johnny

What did Johnny change? He:

- Grouped the actions according to category (one about voting; one about the client list)
- Made the next steps easy (log on to portal, agree list, email list)
- Used strong verbs: 'log on', 'vote', 'agree', 'email'
- Gave clear, separate instructions for each action

Makeover 4: The Great British Email

EXAMPLE: BEFORE

To: Clara

From: Paul

Re: Movers and Shakers

Hello Clara

How are you today? What wonderful weather we're having – I hope you're managing to get out and enjoy it!

Last week I had a meeting with your supplier Movers and Shakers, whom I was extremely impressed by. I was wondering, if you aren't too busy, if you might consider a quick phone conversation with me to discuss your experiences of working with them on your latest project. Of course, if you have too much on right now, I will completely understand – I know that it's a busy period for you with year-end coming up.

Warm wishes,

Paul

What's wrong with it?

It couldn't be less direct if it tried! Paul's trying to be polite and respectful, but actually he's making it harder for Clara to figure out what on earth he actually wants. And so unknowingly, he's not being respectful of her time.

This kind of apologetic language is often used by the British ('I'm sorry I even exist'), but many cultures adopt it when they feel worried about asking for something.

If you give your reader too much of an 'out' ('You're probably really busy', 'Don't want to bother you', etc), then you're giving them a reason not to reply. And they'll probably take you up on it.

You don't have extra-sensory perception – you don't know what they're up to, so don't mention it in your email.

EXAMPLE: AFTER

To: Clara

From: Paul

Re: Movers and Shakers – pick your brains?

Hello Clara

Hope you're enjoying this lovely weather.

Last week I met with your supplier Movers and Shakers – very impressive. I'd be grateful if we could chat briefly about your experiences of working with them.

How is Monday at 10am or 2pm for a ten-min phone call?

Warm wishes,

Paul

What did Paul change? He:

- Reduced the hook to a single sentence
- Cut out waffle ('I was wondering, if you aren't too busy') and apologetic over-politeness
- Offered specific times for the call, making the next step easy
- Included an assertive, but still polite CTA which gets right to the point

So, now you've learned how to make the next step easy and conquered your CTA, you're going to be unstoppable!

But even the best emails sometimes don't get a reply and we need to send a follow-up. Join me in the next chapter to learn how to do that without ever writing 'Just checking in...' again.

TRY IT TODAY

- Ask for one thing per email.
- Be direct with your request.
- Offer a clear timeframe.

11

YOUR SUBJECT LINE
HOLDS *ALL* THE POWER

Three things guaranteed to make me fall asleep:

1. The sound of gently lapping waves

2. A long bath with lavender oil

3. Emails with the subject line 'FYI'

Are you the same? Other subject lines with the *snoresome* effect include:

- February newsletter (yawwwwn)

- Feedback request (eyelids drooping)

- A message from our CEO (head nodding)

- Meeting request (eyes closed)

- Update (deep, deep sleep)

- No action required (Get the crash cart)

You see the problem with most subject lines? They're boring and generic. They don't make you *feel* anything (apart from sleepy). And they don't give you much of an indication of what's to come.

Generic subject lines can also make search a nightmare – the email might include important information that you need the recipients to refer back to, but its generic title makes it impossible to find in the future.

And the biggest problem of all? If emails don't stand out – they don't get opened. You are judged within a nanosecond.

A good subject line does two things that get people cracking open your email as fast as a bottle of beer on a Friday night.

1. It makes the reader feel something:

- Excitement
- Curiosity
- A sense of urgency
- Empathy
- Relief
- Anticipation
- Eagerness
- Delight
- Fear (of missing out, of not opening the email, etc)

This emotional connection is the key to get people to open your email.

2. It makes the reader do something.

A curious subject line gets people to open the email and/ or gets them to do something straight away. Yes, your whole email can be in the subject line. I'll show you how in a moment.

You may have written an email that's punchier than a heavyweight boxer and tighter than your waistband after Christmas, but call it 'Invoice' and you might as well give up.

No one will read your email if your subject line sucks.

So don't dash it off at the start of your email without thinking. Give it proper attention and love at the end.

Subject lines are appetisers.

If your email itself is the hamburger, then think of your subject line as an amuse-bouche – the little pre-morsel that gives an enticing flavour of what's to come. It should be so tasty, it makes your reader want to open and gobble up the rest of your email.

Subject

Six tasty techniques to get your emails opened

1. When you need to get feedback on a document

Try one of these laser-focused subject lines:

- Board report – data for section 5?
- Quick question on slides 12–15.
- Your advice on proposal – 15 mins max!

Why they work:

They're specific so the task feels smaller and more manageable than if you'd asked for 'feedback' or a 'review'.

'Advice' works much better than 'feedback' if you want a response, because it makes your reader feel important.

---

2. When you need a meeting with someone you don't know well

Try one of these intriguing lines:

- Katie Jones reckoned we share an interest in...
- Your LinkedIn post – question on...
- Your take on brand purpose?

Why they work:

They harness the curiosity factor with the ellipsis (...) *and* they focus on the recipient, not on you.

3. When you need to remind someone to do something

Try one of these action lines:

- Sarah – send slides by Tues am pls
- [URGENT] Team – submit self-appraisals by COP today
- Leanne – pls email feedback on Board report by 2pm

Why they work:

They use strong verbs ('send', 'submit', 'email') and are personalised – we home in whenever we see our name. They convey a sense of urgency.

4. When you need to get important information out quickly and clearly

Try one of these all-in-one lines (you may not need the rest of the email):

- Cancelled: 2pm call w/Megacorp
- Croissants in kitchen – help yourself!
- Change of venue: lunch now at Harry's

Why they work:

They lead with the most important point – the change of venue, cancellation and croissants. Who wouldn't want to read about croissants?

5. When you need someone to do something they don't want to do

Try a what's-in-it-for-them line like:

- Get paid faster!
- Five-min review needed (then Project X can get signed off)
- Quick favour to ask (and great news)

Why they work:

They make the action feel easy and show the benefit to the recipient of taking the next step.

6. When you'd normally write FYI

By the way – never do that.

First – do you need to send this email at all? And/ or do you need to send it to everyone on your list?

If you decide it is important, think about what you want the recipient to know or do, and put *that* in the subject line. If this is evergreen information that people will need to refer to in the future, make sure your title relates specifically to the content. For example:

- Exec decision on recruitment – what you need to know
- Five-min read: why appraisal process is changing
- Meeting with Megacorp: highlights

Why they work:

They give a flavour of what's to come in the rest of the email and show the reader how they'll benefit from reading on.

These days, most email platforms organise conversations in threads according to their subject lines. So, try not to change the subject line unless you absolutely have to.

But if the topic changes dramatically from the original conversation, then it's a good idea to start a new thread with a fresh subject line (as long as you say that's what you're doing).

ONLY IN CASE OF EMERGENCY

Reply All

BREAK GLASS

The tyranny of 'reply all'

Nothing tends to make people angrier than when their inbox suddenly fills with fifty-eight emails from people 'replying all' to specify whether they want the chicken, fish or vegetarian option for the holiday party.

Use your reply-all button behind glass that should only be cracked open in case of emergency, ie when absolutely everyone on the email needs to know everything you write.

If your message is just for the sender, simply hit 'reply'. Never hit reply all and type:

- Thanks!
- Congratulations!
- Adding Paul (when there are already fifty people on the email and you're on your 276th message of the thread. You need a call or a meeting at this point).
- Vegetarian, please.

If you need extra incentive to avoid hitting the reply-all button, here's a compelling reason.

British people send
a whopping

64m

unnecessary emails,
every single day!

If every UK adult sent one
fewer 'thank you' email every
day, we would save more than

16,433
tonnes

of carbon a year...

...that's equivalent to

81,152

flights to Madrid,

or taking

3,334

diesel cars off the road!

Source: OVO Energy

A study by energy company OVO found that in the UK, we send a whopping 64 m unnecessary emails every day.[8] It reckons if every adult in the UK sent one fewer 'thank you' email a day, we would save more than 16,433 tonnes of carbon a year – equivalent to 81,152 flights to Madrid or taking 3,334 diesel cars off the road.

Wow.

So remember: send fewer emails, save the planet and make sure the ones you *do* send get opened with an enticing subject line.

TRY IT TODAY

- The all-in-one subject line to get straight to the point.
- Use your recipient's name to get their attention straight away.
- Use action words like 'reply' and 'read'.

---

8   'Think before you thank': If every Brit sent one less thank you email a day, we would save 16,433 tonnes of carbon a year – the same as 81,152 flights to Madrid' (OVO, 2019), www.ovoenergy.com/ovo-newsroom/press-releases/2019/november/think-before-you-thank-if-every-brit-sent-one-less-thank-you-email-a-day-we-would-save-16433-tonnes-of-carbon-a-year-the-same-as-81152-flights-to-madrid.html, accessed October 2020

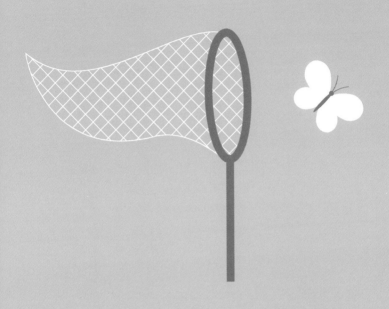

12

NO MORE 'JUST CHECKING IN' – A FOLLOW-UP MASTERCLASS

My friend Helen told me this hilarious story recently when we were chatting about follow-up.

She'd been asking her dad for some time about the wellbeing of an elderly relative whom she'd written to a few times, but who hadn't replied.

Her father ended up hiring a private detective to see if he could trace what was going on. The report came back to say that the elderly relative was still living at the same address she'd lived at for fifty years.

After some questioning, my friend found out her dad had actually had the relative's phone number all along, but 'didn't want to bother her'. He'd hired a private detective just to avoid feeling like a nuisance.

An actual private detective.

Let that sink in for a moment.

The softly-softly approach

But my friend's dad isn't as unusual as he might seem. We're hardwired to *not* bother people, aren't we? We don't want to pester or annoy people. No one wants to be a nag or be seen as a snoop.

It applies to how we manage our emails, too.

We pussyfoot around the issue and send 'softly-softly' follow-up emails like:

- Just checking in to see if you've had a chance to read my report?

- I know you're extremely busy right now, but I wanted see how those figures are coming along, if you've had time to look at them at all?

- Sorry to bother you, but I just wondered if you've been able to disarm the bomb I told you about last week?

They're meant to soften the blow so people don't get annoyed. But in reality, they don't convey enough urgency to get the recipient to act.

The passive-aggressive (or just plain aggressive) approach

If we've skipped breakfast and feel a little cranky, we might go in with the more passive-aggressive starter: 'As per my last email...' This roughly translates as 'Argh! I've had it with your $%!^'.

Or we try a 'friendly reminder', which of course is about as friendly as a dose of measles.

Passive-aggressive language lays down a big ol' guilt trip on your reader. It makes them 1) feel bad about themselves and 2) want to avoid the person who makes them feel bad about themselves – *you*!

No one wants to be reminded of the fact that they haven't done something. So ditch language like 'Further to my email of 25 April' or 'I've written to you on fifty-eight previous occasions' if you want to get a reply.

And remember – you don't know what's going on in someone else's life. They might have fallen ill, suffered a bereavement or have another good reason for not replying to your email. So play nice.

The most annoying phrases used in work emails[9]

- Not sure if you saw my last email... 25%

- Per my last email... 13%

- Per our conversation... 11%

- Any updates on this? 11%

- Sorry for the double email 10%

- Please advise 9%

- As previously stated... 6%

- As discussed... 6%

- Re-attaching for convenience 6%

---

9   '2018 Adobe Consumer Email Survey' (Adobe, 2018), www.slideshare.net/adobe/2018-adobe-consumer-email-survey, accessed October 2018

The four steps for successful follow-up

 ### 1. Go back to the scene of the crime

Take a look at your original email with fresh eyes. Did you use your HEC Hamburger Technique? Did it have a seductive subject line and a clear CTA with a deadline?

Chances are, you might not have made the next steps easy enough for your reader.

If you missed a key piece of information like a deadline or a specific action, rewrite the email and send it afresh with a PS or intro saying something like 'Resending this request with more detail to make it easier for you.'

If you keep on forwarding the same rubbish email, you'll get the same rubbish results.

2. Step away from the keyboard

Ask yourself if email really is the best method for your follow-up.

We tend to default to email follow-up without thinking through other options. (Remember Chapter 1, how we're often on autopilot?)

A simple phone call can work wonders.

I've lost count of the times clients have complained to me that they haven't been able to get a reply from someone despite months of trying and 'countless' emails.

I tell them to pick up the phone.

One phone call later, they get hold of the person immediately and resolve the outstanding issue in just a couple of minutes. (They're normally pretty sheepish at this point that they wasted so much time.)

Why do phone calls work so well?

Well, they allow you to get to the bottom of the radio silence.

Maybe there was a simple reason, like the recipient was too busy to reply. But perhaps it was subtler than that – like they did actually look at your proposal, but thought it was too expensive. Or they didn't give you feedback on your deck because they're secretly mad at you for not inviting them to the exec meeting.

It's much easier to immediately uncover any underlying issues like these on the phone, when you get to hear someone's tone of voice.

If you're phone phobic (as many people are now that we use our phones more for messaging and less for talking), think about other channels you might use instead of emailing again: instant messaging, texting, direct messaging via social media, etc.

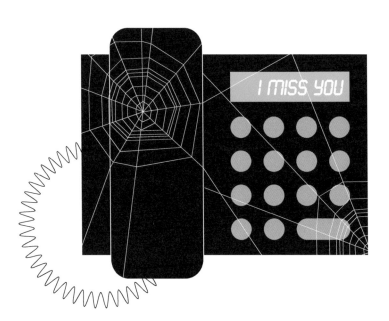

When NOT to email

1. **When you've sent more than one follow-up email asking someone for something.** Really, one is enough.

2. **When someone's sent you a negative or critical email.** An email reply often adds petrol to the fire (see Chapter 2). Picking up the phone at this point can make an enormous difference and often elicits an apology from the other person rather than a confrontation. Try it!

3. **When your email is turning into a Netflix mini-series.** If you're trying to communicate complex information, ask yourself if a quick call would speed things up. Ten minutes on the phone might persuade the recipient more easily than your 500-word email (that they probably won't even read).

4. **When you've screwed up.** Saying 'I'm sorry' is generally best done face to face or over the phone. Emails can give the impression of avoidance and an inauthentic apology comes across badly.

5. **When someone phones you a lot.** I had a client who rarely emailed, and instead phoned me. I always made an effort to ring her as much as possible instead of emailing. It was clearly her preferred way of doing business and it cemented our relationship with every call.

3. Use your two-syllable secret

If email follow-up is your best or only option, here's an essential tip for you. The word 'because' is a miracle worker when it comes to getting people to act. Studies show we're conditioned to comply when people give us a reason, however spurious it is.[10]

Need to get clients to process dull paperwork? Give them a reason why ('Because it means we won't have to keep pestering you for information all the time').

Want to get invoices paid? Tell clients why prompt payment is so important to you ('Because it means we can pay our suppliers faster and get your project finished quicker').

4. Craft a clever follow-up

OK – time to write! Use everything you've learned so far, think about your audience, your HEC Hamburger and subject-line techniques, and craft a thoughtful, guilt-free follow-up.

---

10   RB Cialdini, *Influence: The psychology of persuasion* (Harper Business, 2007)

Try this on for size:

EXAMPLE

To: Hamid

From: Celine

Re: 20 mins in your diary (max, I promise!)

Hi Hamid

I know you're up to your eyeballs with year-end reporting, so I'll make this quick.

I need 20 mins with you this week to get your feedback on the branding project. This is so we can launch in time for our annual conference.

Does Wednesday am or Thursday pm work for a quick phone chat?

Best wishes,

Celine

Why this works:

- It uses informal, human language that empathises with Hamid's situation (no guilt trip).

- It reiterates *why* he should act ('so we can launch in time for our annual conference').

- It has a *clear, easy next step* – the twenty-minute phone chat is offered as an easier alternative than email feedback.

- It doesn't dwell on the negatives (that Hamid hasn't responded previously), but instead *focuses on a positive future* for everyone (launching on time).

Variations for your follow-up

You can also include one or more of these three methods:

- Offer an alternative to move forward in a less time-intensive way for your recipient:

  » If filling out the questionnaire feels like too much of a headache right now, how about we jump on a ten-minute call on Friday afternoon?

  » If your plate's too full at the moment and you'd rather revisit this next month, just hit reply and say 'Next month'.

  » Let me know if you need me to follow up with one of your colleagues/ team instead to get this information.

- Make an assumptive close:

  » If I don't hear back by Friday, I'll assume it's a no for now.

  » If I don't hear from you by the end of the week, I'll assume you're OK with this final draft.

- Be funny:

  » Hi – it's your annoyingly cheerful colleague seeing if we can get this meeting in the diary.

  » Did you get buried under a pile of unpaid invoices?

» I realise I'm a pain in the backside for asking, but a quick reply would make my day!

Psst! Don't forget a sensational subject line

Go back to Chapter 11 to make sure you use the *right subject line for your follow-up* too.

'Checking in' or 'Following up' will likely just be ignored.

A guilt trip title like 'Resending email of 29 April' makes people feel bad *and* they'll ignore you.

Forwarding your last lame email with no change of title (eg just 'Fwd: Feedback required') reminds the recipient that they haven't done something that they didn't want to do first time round and *still* don't want to do. Then they'll ignore you all over again.

So which subject lines do work for follow-up? You could try:

- Humorous questions: 'Was my last email so good you fainted?'; 'Can't get enough of my graphs?' It puts your reader at ease immediately and takes away any guilt. (You may be surprised at how well humour works in emails – try it.)

- Statements with a timescale: 'Just 43 secs of your time!' The recipient is more likely to reply if it looks like a small job.

- Subject lines with a reason: 'Need your comments today to stay on print schedule.'

So there you have it. The secrets of brilliant email follow-up (the secret often being don't email at all).

TRY IT TODAY

- Pick up the phone instead of emailing and see what results you get.
- Use humour in your follow-ups when it's appropriate.
- Include your secret weapon, 'because', to share the rationale behind your request.

13

READ THIS BEFORE
YOU HIT SEND

Now that you've written such an awesome email, I bet you're itching to hit send. You want your beautifully crafted piece of art to go out into the world to see what bounty it brings back.

I get it.

But if you don't review and edit your email, you risk undoing all your great work.

A slip of the keyboard and a missing 'l' in public can be devastating.

Even the White House isn't immune to a typo: one statement called for 'peach' in the Middle East. The internet is littered with these cringey mistakes.

But, you may ask, a little typo can't hurt that much, can it?

While typos might seem harmless, they have a big impact. Research shows they make us appear less intelligent than we are.

We get all judgy when it comes to other people's grammar, too. Online dating site Match.com surveyed 5,509 single Americans,[11] finding that 39% judged the suitability of candidates by their grasp of grammar. This made it more important than their dress sense or even (gasp) their teeth.

11   'Singles in America: Match releases largest study on U.S. single population' (Match.com, 2017), https://match.mediaroom.com/2017-02-06-Singles-in-America-Match-Releases-Largest-Study-on-U-S-Single-Population, accessed October 2020

Five final steps to finesse your emails

 ## 1. Say it loud and proud

Read your email out loud. This allows you to check:

- Tone (do I sound like a real person, or a corporate robot?)
- Sentence length (are they short enough that I can say them in one breath?)
- Interest levels (if you get bored reading it, your reader will too)
- Missing words/typos/grammatical errors (when we read in our head, we tend to skip ahead and miss mistakes)

 ## 2. Chop, chop

Most of your emails should be eighty words max – that's around five sentences. Ideally, they'd be shorter. So do a word count and get your scissors out (aka your delete key) if you need to.

If you struggle to strip back your word count, revisit the advice from Chapter 9 and see what you can chop. Maybe all you really need is a quick CTA. Or even just a subject line.

Remember to check for:

- Filler words (definitely, very, just, that, etc)
- Waffle (only critical info needed)
- Relevance (ask 'Who cares?' after every paragraph)

 ## 3. Hone your hamburger

Do you have a hook, explanation and clear CTA?

 ## 4. Make sure it looks mighty fine

Remember to appeal to your reader's eyes.

Check for:

- Line spacing (not too squished)
- Bolding (to highlight key points)
- Bullets (for lists)
- White space (lots of it)
- Attachments (did I remember to attach them?)

5. Don't trust that evil mastermind (your spell check)

The spellchecker on your phone or computer is far from infallible. In fact, it can make things worse by replacing words you *had* actually intended to use.

Plug-ins like Grammarly can help dramatically with picking up both spelling and grammatical errors (you're vs your; it's vs its are common mistakes). But there's no substitute for a proper proofread.

To find errors, try:

- Reading your email backwards.
- Temporarily changing the font, size and colour of your text. This can move the words around so you feel like you're looking at a brand-new email with fresh eyes.

And finally, no, you can't have one of those butt-covering email signatures that says 'Sent on the move – please excuse typos, etc.' People will still think you're slapdash. *Even if you've got great teeth.*

TRY IT TODAY

- Read your email out loud before sending to highlight any clunky parts.

- Cut out filler words like 'definitely' and 'just'.

- Read it backwards to sniff out typos.

CONCLUSION

YOUR SEVEN-DAY EPIC
EMAIL CHALLENGE

So here we are, at the end of this small but mighty book. Sniff.

You've learned that brilliant email writing is all about understanding people – getting inside their heads and out of yours.

You've discovered how to be more persuasive by showing what's in it for them.

And you've learned how to make it easy for them to reply to you and give you what you want.

Feels good, right?

But, of course, knowledge is just the first step. Perfect emails aren't made overnight – you now need to practise.

Make like a mad scientist

 Now's the time to put on your lab coat and get experimenting. I want you to get cracking and concoct a variety of emails and see what potently persuasive potions *you* can come up with.

 Test various hooks and see which ones work best for your audience.

 Investigate different CTAs and discover which gets the fastest/ best response.

Trial several sign-offs for different audiences to see which works and when.

With practice, you'll soon see that even small tweaks to your emails can bring powerful results:

- **Faster responses** (because you're making the next step clear)

- **Less chasing** (no more 'Just checking in...' or 'As per my last email')

- **Better engagement** (because you've removed that stick from up your backside and ditched the corporate speak)

- **More time to focus on actual work** (you're waaaaay more productive now that you can inspire people to do what you want)

The challenge

Over the next seven days, I want you to send out one of each of these three emails using the techniques in this book to make them irresistible:

The enticing introduction

Email someone new to introduce yourself, your business or your services. You need to get their attention, show why they should care and be clear on what you need from them.

✕

Email of *Excellence*

To
_____

CC/BCC
_____

Subject
_____

Send

The confident CTA

Get someone to do something for you: give you a referral, an introduction, a favour, some feedback; review a document; agree to a meeting, etc. Use all your tools of persuasion and make the next step easy by being explicit about what they need to do.

The feisty follow-up

You haven't had a reply to the email you sent two weeks ago and you need an answer? Send a fantastic follow-up with all the tips you learned in Chapter 12 so you can get a response fast and move forward.

Good luck – you're going to be great.

And remember: the more emails you write, the better you'll get.

Hit me up!

After you've finished your challenge, drop me a line to kim@kimarnold.co.uk and let me know how you got on. I can't wait to hear your success stories and case studies.

Or tweet me at @kimarnold5 or connect with me on LinkedIn: karnoldcomms.

There's more...

As an extra bonus for you, go to kimarnold.co.uk/email-attraction to download your free one-page Epic Email checklist.

Refer to this indispensable checklist every time you write an email, to make sure you have all the vital ingredients, the right tone and a killer CTA.

It condenses your HEC Hamburger Technique and all the other tasty titbits from this book into an easily digested bite-sized mouthful. It's your shortcut to getting your email opened and answered and the results you need.

Enjoy!

Download yours now at kimarnold.co.uk/email-attraction.

ACKNOWLEDGEMENTS

First up, my hilarious, big-brained coach, mentor and friend, Kim Duke. Thank you for alternately holding my hand and kicking my butt throughout the writing process. (Even the 'WANT TO STICK A FORK IN MY EYE – REWRITE!' comments in my early drafts.)

To my awesomely talented illustrator, Emma-Jane Black. Thank you for turning my rambling briefs into mini masterpieces. The world needs to see more of your work. (Contact Emma on helloemmablack@gmail.com.)

To my wonderful clients who've generously let me into their inboxes over the years and worked so hard to transform their emails. You've inspired so many of the makeovers included in this book.

To my business bestie Antonia – your proofing, PR wisdom and chat were a godsend (oh, and the cocktails too).

To my awesome assistant, Sarah Begley, for your calm, methodical support when my head was too full to think straight.

To the team at Rethink Press for guiding me through the publishing process so brilliantly.

To my mum, dad and brother, for always believing in me (even when I didn't).

And finally to Felix, my biggest fan (height wise, at least). Thank you for your unerring kindness, support, wise counsel and cups of tea. You are the best.

THE AUTHOR

International business communication consultant and speaker Kim Arnold shows people how to get noticed, make their messages stick and be remembered (in all the right ways). She's allergic to bad emails, and stuffy phrases like 'Herewith please find attached' make her come out in hives.

Kim helps people avoid the wasted time and effort associated with poor communication. She helps the world's leading organisations – including FTSE 250 businesses, international banks, global law firms, tech scale-ups and more – transform their communication, marketing and branding, connect with their audience and get the results they need.

Kim is a panel tutor at the University of Cambridge's Institute of Continuing Education, where she teaches marketing and branding. She lives in London, England, with her giant husband and two children.

Kim has been a Prince's Trust Mentor, so 10% of the proceeds from this book will go to this youth charity, helping young people get into jobs, education and training.

Email Kim at kim@kimarnold.co.uk to find out about:

- **Writing and communication masterclasses** perfect for helping teams win people over with their words
- **Energising keynotes** to show large groups how to stand out and be heard (both online and in real life)
- **Consultancy** for particular communication gremlins (like conveying technical information, describing your services in less than 10,000 words or engaging stakeholders)
- **1:1 coaching** to help you become a supercommunicator

Sign up for Kim's weekly communication tips and find out more at: www.kimarnold.co.uk.

Connect with her on social media:

- karnoldcomms
- @kimarnold5
- @wordsdonewell
- @kimarnoldcomms

Printed in Great Britain
by Amazon

26580253R00098